WHAT THE WILLOW SAID

AS IT FELL

What the willow said as it fell

Andrea Scarpino

 RED HEN PRESS | PASADENA, CA

Book layout by Nicole Younce

Library of Congress Cataloging-in-Publication Data

Names: Scarpino, Andrea, author.
Title: What the willow said as it fell / Andrea Scarpino.
Description: Pasadena, CA : Red Hen Press, 2016.
Identifiers: LCCN 2015050379 | ISBN 9781597097314 (paperback)
Subjects: LCSH: Human body—Poetry. | Chronic pain—Poetry. | BISAC: POETRY /
   General.
Classification: LCC PS3619.C275 W48 2016 | DDC 811/.6—dc23
LC record available at http://lccn.loc.gov/2015050379

The National Endowment for the Arts, the Los Angeles County Arts Commission, the Los Angeles Department of Cultural Affairs, the Dwight Stuart Youth Fund, the Pasadena Arts & Culture Commission and the City of Pasadena Cultural Affairs Division, Sony Pictures Entertainment, and Ahmanson Foundation partially support Red Hen Press.

First Edition
Published by Red Hen Press
www.redhen.org

Acknowledgments

Scientific and medical information, poetic lines, definitions, and personal reflections are borrowed and included in italics from the following sources: Sir Astley Paston Cooper, *On the Anatomy of the Breast*; Brian Teare, *Sight Map*; Carrie Shipers, *Cause for Concern*; Elaine Scarry, *The Body in Pain*; Florence Williams, *Breasts: A Natural and Unnatural History*; Hayden Herrera, *Frida Kahlo: The Paintings*; Laurie Edwards, *In the Kingdom of the Sick*; Lynne Greenberg, *The Body Broken*; Melanie Thernstrom, *The Pain Chronicles*; Olavi Huikari, *The Miracle of Trees*; Sarah E. Prance and Helen A. Pass, "Etiology and Management of Breast Pain," (*Advanced Therapy of Breast Disease*); Susie Orbach, *Bodies* and "There is No Such Thing as a Body" (*The British Journal of Psychotherapy*, September 2003); Tom Junod, "Theater of Pain," (*Esquire* magazine, February 2013); *Oxford English Dictionary*; and *Self* Magazine's October 2012 issue, particularly "Too Young for Cancer." I am grateful to the editors of *Barnstorm Literary Journal*, *Red Earth Review*, *Stone Canoe*, and *The Burden of Light: Poems on Illness and Loss* who published excerpts from this book, often in very different versions.

Many, many people helped shape and encourage this book, in many ways. I am deeply grateful for Tracy Brain and Gerard Woodward for guiding my writing throughout my PhD at Bath Spa University. This book wouldn't exist without them. Thank you, as well, to David Harsent, Carrie Etter, and Tim Middleton, and to my fellow students at BSU, particularly Helen Storey, who provided much needed encouragement, critical readings, and trips to the pub. And a special thank you to Philip Gross and Samantha Walton who kindly guided me through my Viva.

I am indebted to Phil Cogley for teaching me how to loop, and to Chris Bobel, Norma Jenckes, Lois Melina, Loree Miltich, Larry Preston, and Saara Myrene Raappana for reading drafts of this work in various stages of completion and providing wonderfully helpful feedback.

And to Carrie Shipers and Jennifer Smith, my first readers extraordinaire, "thank you" is too small and never enough. But thank you, again and again.

I am incredibly thankful to many friends/family, too many to list, who have supported me in writing this book. Thank you, always.

And to Zac. Everything.

For Zac

What the willow said

as it fell

Our bodies, I learned, are not temples.
They are more like trees.

—Florence Williams

Because in times like these
to have you listen at all, it's necessary
to talk about trees.

—Adrienne Rich

Before the day :

sunrise over the lake,
seagull clatter, crow,

sound of glasses stacked,
restacked, metal slid

into place. Cacophony
of blossoming :

forsythia, lilac, cherry's
pink-tipped sway.

How long has the body
refused sleep? Damp hand

of the sheet startling.

      Hours
      months
      years?

Time moves slowly.

Before the day
the body feels its way

into shape :   almost risen
body   almost in pain.

Love

early spring morning,
we walked the lake trail,

cool sand, red pine grove.
Church bells rang the hour,

someone played bagpipes,
a slow lament, dirt thrown

on a grave. Or was it
the trees?

Crow calling his mate?
Time moved slowly.

How long had
everything died inside me

and rotted there,
white stains on the ultrasound :

cysts the size of   peas
                         almonds
                         apricots.

White stains where pain
breaks through wet earth,

unfolds, extends.
We walked the lake trail—

church bells, bagpipes—
and you knelt among new ferns

to lace your shoe.
Wasps rose

from the ground
a yellow swarm—

                your hands
                to mouth   eyes—

as you knelt on their nest—

                you must have knelt
                on their nest—

your hands to   nose
                     ears
                     throat

your face alive with sting   swarm
beating wings.

And I walked

                    away

told you

                    to walk away—

Come to me
again and again.

And you did.

And the wasps
stayed with their nest.

Love
this is the body in pain :

                    spring opened
                    in our lungs—
                    a sudden swarm
                    hands at your face.

This is the body
searching—

How desperate she is—

excise the   pain
                          poisoning—

                          scalpel
                          surgical hook—

layers of flesh   cut
                          exposed

                          freed—

Ashes to ashes—

I reached for your face—

It all began with   a strange collision   there were no tears
and a handrail pierced me the way   a sword pierces a bull
tremendous hemorrhage   spinal column broken   pelvis
two ribs   cutting and cutting of bones
The first thing I thought   a bolero   with pretty colors
I got a little better with the corset   but now feel just as sick
a frightful pain   in my lungs   I can hardly walk   sleep
I live in a painful planet   transparent as ice   a fearful
kind of mystery   punishment   The dove made a mistake
I have been sick a year   four months   eight months bedridden
I do not see anything   that improves my condition
I am so often alone   a weariness   desperation
no words can describe   bland   lucid   old—

Before the day :

moon a gaping mouth,
sunburned grass, bindweed.

Time moved slowly.
Storms gathered in the east,

bent branches low to the ground,
ash rooted darkness,

gathered breath in its leaves,
glint of golden offering.

Before the day :

lightning, one long, loud crack.
And ash collapsed, a splintering,

crown in orange flames,
soot raining. Ozone hung in the air.

And our bodies rose,
arms like wind through leaves,

hair like spring's wild blossoming,
our hearts' growth rings, root-veins—

nerve trees, lymphatic tree—
pulse of nerve   to spinal cord   to brain.

In the meadow's blackened opening,
our bodies rose from ash, burning—

Tell me, is pain the garden's only plan?

Humans share 50% of our DNA with trees   ribbons of living tissue
epidermis   cuticle cortex   vascular cambium   heartwood
root hairs   mother cells   leaves that breathe
male and female hormones :   ash changes sex   different branches
The same substances   work on   the human nervous system   trees
can be put to sleep   chloroform and ether   telegraph system
initiates defenses   under duress :   jasmonic acid   ethylene
Trees may not feel   pity   and   pain?—

Before the day :

a baby born
with damaged lungs—

body its own landscape,
valleys, marshes, mountain peaks.

Body its own mooring. Sea.
And her mother swaddled her

in bright blankets,
passed her through a split

in ash's trunk, praying,
Take this body. Make it whole.

And ash did, filled the baby's lungs,
blushed her skin with oxygen.

So other mothers came,
brought babies with colic, fever,

babies who wouldn't eat :

      ashes
      through
      ash tree.

One by one, healed—

What is remembered in the body
        is well remembered—

Decades passed. Centuries.
Time moved slowly.

Then, one day, the borers came,
an iridescent green bulleting

through bark, shade-filled canopies.

One by one, ash starved,
a slow withering.

And the trees closed forever—

So Mother came with me,
child body its own landscape,

uncontained wildfire
              pained—

No miracle. Too late.

Because the borers came,
always to suffer. Always to break—

Ms. Scarpino is a   pleasant 35-year-old patient   from Marquette, Michigan
well dressed today   appropriate   speech normal   rate and tone
given her history   underlying hypersensitivity   stimuli from
non-damaging causes   interpreted as pain   my exam does not duplicate
discomfort   she is becoming   more and more frustrated   unable
to tell   what will aggravate symptoms   not opposed to
bilateral mastectomy   how desperate she is
Ms. Scarpino is a delightful 33-year-old   clean   casual appearance
few pain behaviors   good eye contact   orientation to person   place
and time   mood   a little dysphoric   no suicide ideation
all hormones within normal range   recent breast imaging evaluation
negative for cancer   Patient is 30 years old   no evident distress
red cell morphology   abnormal   another hemoglobin abnormality
may be present   Ms. Scarpino is 28 years old   unspecified endocrine disorder
other signs and symptoms   in the breast   evident
bilateral clubfoot deformity   surgical correction   during infancy
On physical examination   patient is pleasant female   20 years of age
breasts without abnormalities   scars on the Achilles
bilateral pronation   normal gait   Thalassemia minor
This is the rheumatology-rehabilitation consultation on   a 14-year-old
diagnosed   reflex sympathetic dystrophy   stage IV
patient   frequent episodes
headache   canker sores   chest pain—

Pain (n).
(classical Latin) :

> punishment, penalty,
> *suffering or loss inflicted*

> *for a crime, offence;*
> *thought to be endured*

> *by souls in hell;*
> *mental distress or suffering;*

> *annoying or tiresome*
> *person or thing—*

As in :

pain-dimmed
pain-drawn
pain-chastened
pain-shot
pain-wrung—

As in :

Mastalgia (n).
(ancient Greek) *(rare before mid-twentieth century)* :

    one or both   breasts—

    Nights I couldn't sleep,
    lay awake imagining

    knife point to flesh—

    days through meadow,
    red pine grove,

    each step sounding.

    As in mastectomy—
    How desperate she is—

As in :

Blood's backward flow
a fluttering,

mitral valve   open
                          closed
                          leaking.

Her surgeon hands traced
each sketch.

The heart so beautiful,
all these branches.

Arborescent—

Ash, I said
under my breath.

Because the borers came—

As in :

Pain begets pain   body increasingly   responsive
pressure   light touch   a broken alarm signaling
its brokenness   No one etiologic factor   identified :   subtle
hormonal variations   end-organ sensitivity   altered local receptors
complex interactions   in the brain   Most pain resolves
promptly   once stimulus removed   and body healed   Chronic pain
extends   beyond—   a bifurcation :
where you used to live   the new disease of pain
the body as pleasure   changes   haunted   persecuted
easier to be alone   no one healthy can understand—

As in :

Fans know nothing   the work   the rehab
getting   out of bed   Monday morning
People ask   "Are you feeling good?"   No
you never feel good   knee   rib   shoulder
ankle   back   wrist   head
ten times   one hundred times   crippling
When you always   hurt   how do you know?
until   you stand up to walk   and can't walk
try to run   and can't
body immobilized   strapped to a board   carried away
Pain offers   the quickest   respect
quality of player   quality of person
Fear fused   by pain   and blood
If you can go   you go   hit anything that moves—

As in :

I didn't have a family history   never missed a checkup
My gynecologist   rubbed my back   said my hormones
were out of balance   I was stressed   overworked
crazy   needed to lose weight   kept prescribing antibiotics
inhalers   Xanax   skin bloody
from scratching   night sweats   fever
dark purple bruises   persistent cough   abnormal bleeding
headaches   I could feel a tumor   inside me
for a year   I felt like I had the flu   symptoms
for seven months   three months   two years
Forget early detection   already spread   lungs
spinal cord   brain   two weeks from my 24th birthday
The doctor   had never before seen cancer   with her naked eye
I want to live the life   of a person my age
I had the urge to drive   as far and as fast   as I could—

As in :

fourth floor office,
thick window panes.

Something drew your eye—
flash of her winter coat?—

and you turned your head
to see a woman step

into the road.
One foot on the curb

and then—

Could you have heard car brakes?
Thud of body against machine?

The driver pulled her from
wheel well. Wind shook

the window frames.
Something drew your eye—

the need for someone to see?

Later, you asked me
What would make someone—?

Love

*Pain changes us
and everything we touch—*

Nights I lay awake,
days through meadow,

red pine grove—

Changes us:
we touch something

inside ourselves
we never want to touch.

Once, I found myself screaming,
beating the bedroom door with fists

and feet, Mother locked inside
distracting Brother from my screams.

Found myself weeping.
Child body its own landscape :

pain spread

       foot to knee
       hip
       stomach

       skin

       bruised green
       yellow
       black.

Crutches, wheelchair, spinal taps,
intravenous chemical cocktails.

I screamed at the bedroom door,
hammer-struck my hands.

Everything my child body touched—

Once, I found myself imagining
knife point, blade carving flesh from bone :

       bread's   serrated edge
       paring's   nimbleness.

I slept and woke to them,
black handles in a row.

How one would slice cleanly,
another leave a scar like teeth

had bit into my chest,
sucked away the poisoning.

Pain changes us—

      knife point warmed
      on the stove—

and everything we touch :

      blood in the sink,
      skin raised—

When you always hurt—

Before the day :

sunrise over the lake,
crow chatter, ash tree,

you asleep next to me
dreamless I know because

you never dream.
Hands at your face.

I lie awake—

    say it—

fibrocystic breasts	ovarian cysts	endometriosis
uterine fibroids	polyps	hot flashes
swollen hands	hips	migraine—

I lie awake—

unopposed estrogen	progesterone	perimenopause
hypersensitivity	endocrine disruption	anxiety
unspecified	*signs and symptoms—*	

And what of estrogen? How much is too much?

And what of soy   radiation   plastics?

   1,000 chemicals alter endocrine systems—

phthalates	Bisphenol A	vinyl chloride
dioxin	parabens	styrene
PCB	benzene	flame retardants
DDT	atrazine	lindane
triclosan	cadmium	lead—

Walking in a biochemical wilderness, women's bodies are reacting unpredictably—

The Inuit, whose breast milk could qualify as hazardous waste—

We are the sum of our DNA + chemicals + something else (unspecified) :

early puberty	stress	diet
age of pregnancy	breast density	exercise—

Father	Mother	Aunts
cancer	tumors	pain—

I lie awake.

Calculate   specialists in state after state   *Siren's song of a cure—*

birth control	progesterone cream	acetaminophen
ibuprofen	codeine	vitamin E
B vitamins	omega 3	flax seeds

vitex
iodine swabbed
no soy
carbohydrates
hot water bottles
packs of castor oil
acupuncture
meditation

diuretics
on thighs
caffeine
sugar
ice
cabbage leaves
biofeedback
maca root

cruciferous vegetables
bed rest
dairy
hard exercise
sports bra
lymphatic massage
TENS machine
yoga—

Glint of golden offering—

And what of

Hippocrates :

body will right itself :

primum non nocere—

And what of psychotherapy?

Mother
                  part flesh
                  part metaphor

her child body asleep
against the car door

and the door   unlatched
                  opened—

both hands in the gravel road.

Grandmother grabbed her waist,
her homemade dress,

a yellow cotton flowering,
and pulled her back inside.

Another day
Grandfather passed a truck

with sheets of glass
stacked vertically, rope tied.

Untied.

Glass broke in waves over the car,
cut her thighs, arms.

Blood in her hair, leather seat—

And what of the heart?

The arterial tree from the left heart
branches to supply the body with blood—

They opened his chest,
his heart in their hands pumping.

No longer

pumping.

And what of skin set to flame?
Dog in the road. Reflex : swerve—

arms
where her arms went to her face
burned to bone.

Six months in the hospital,
grafts bathed with nutrients,

antibiotics through ports in her feet.
Skin grew back in darkened ropes.

And what of the girl I loved,
hair like golden leaves,

who wanted to die daily,
cut her arms with knives, razor blades?

Who once told me
You can't trust anyone in this house.

They opened her skull.
Stapled it closed.

And what of ribs picked clean,
a canopy of bone, heart released

from its cage? Up the trail,
one long forelimb, black hoof.

Spring doe, starving,
torn to its parts.

Heart	skin	brain :
part muscle	part metaphor	part pain.

And what of the willow tree?
One hundred years beside the lake.

Girls played in its long-armed cape,
braided branches like hair,

mothers turned its switches into pain.

Mallard ducks, Mute Swans, geese
built nests with matted leaves.

Night of the hurricane, my child body
asleep. Sideways rain, lightning :

one long, loud crack and the willow split
in two, one half in the lake, one half

through the roof, broken windows,
plaster knocked from the walls.

What the willow said as it fell :
Take this body. Make it whole.

And I woke with a crown of leaf
and limb, bark-thickened skin,

sap down my arms—

      salicin :
      aspirin—

What is remembered in the body
is well remembered—

Mother's voice
through my room's darkness :

part crying out, part inhaled breath—

And what of the breast?

Nerves and blood vessels   (in a dried preparation)
show a single lactiferous tube   nipple and areola   numerous
cutaneous glands   magnified four times   injected with red wax
quicksilver   mercury   The gland at eleven months
thirteen years   seventy-three   exhibiting rose-like folds
dorsal nerves   intercostal muscles   ossified branch of an artery
some carbonate   and phosphate of lime
Veins form a circle around the nipple   radiated branches   terminate
Beautiful   Arborescent—

And in what year?

Two decades.

First symptom?

Pain.

And can you describe—?

A lightning strike   jagged
branching :

outer edge of each breast
nipple to rib

then sternum   hips
swollen knees   feet—

And can you describe—?

Abstraction's burn :

pills swallowed without drink—
or drink   and   drink—

sleep   or   no sleep—

Swollen knuckles   fingers   feet
I cannot lift my arms   button closed my blouse   six Motrin
no effect   The sun   a cloudless sky
I want to write its loveliness—   caught   in my chest

                                        What loveliness?

Another treatment   failed :   plastic packs of vitamins
three times daily   high protein diet   omega 3
New specialist :   *Women always respond*   *high rate of success—*
Three months daily   constant   pain
I lie awake   imagine cutting   from my chest   my breasts
the poisoning   knife point to flesh   flesh freed
Called twice   crying   *Stay the course*, his nurses said—

And what does it feel like?

An ache   a burning heat
day breaking into flames

a storm-filled sky   darkening—

No.

A heaviness   swelling
red dust through everything—

No.

A tear   constant.
A razor lodged   each breath—

No.
Pain feels

like nothing except   pain—

And how have you *coped?*

> *(v) to prove oneself a match,*
> *come to blows, engage—*

> specialists in state after state
> hormones
> diet change
> pain killers
> therapy
> days through meadow
> red pine grove—

Mayo Clinic :   red notebook   purple pen
Questions in a column   left hand page   Answers   blank
right hand page :   *all hormones*   *normal range*
Breast specialists   pain specialists   gynecology   endocrinology
internal medicine :   *Unknown cause*   *anomaly*—

And what if I asked—

say it—

mastectomy?

What they tell you isn't right—
Her chest concave,

a shallow bowl
like I'd been hollowed out.

Numb from clavicle to ribs.
They don't just take your breasts.

They change everything—

Pain begets pain begets pain begets pain
begets pain begets pain begets pain begets
pain begets pain begets pain begets pain
begets pain begets pain begets pain begets
pain begets pain begets pain begets pain
begets pain begets pain begets pain begets
pain begets pain begets pain begets pain
begets pain begets pain begets pain begets
pain begets pain begets pain begets pain
begets pain begets pain begets pain begets
pain begets pain begets pain begets pain
begets pain begets pain begets pain begets
pain begets pain begets pain begets pain
begets pain begets pain begets pain begets
pain begets pain begets pain begets pain
begets pain begets pain begets pain begets
pain begets pain begets pain begets pain
begets pain begets pain begets pain begets
pain begets pain begets pain begets pain
begets pain begets pain begets pain begets
pain begets pain begets pain begets pain
begets pain begets pain begets pain begets
pain begets pain begets pain begets pain
begets pain begets pain begets pain begets
pain begets pain begets pain begets pain
begets pain begets pain begets pain begets
pain begets pain begets pain begets pain
begets pain begets pain begets pain begets
pain begets pain begets pain begets pain
begets pain begets pain begets pain begets
pain begets pain begets pain begets pain
begets pain begets pain begets pain begets
pain begets pain begets pain begets pain—

Because the borers came—

No matter how hard I try   the toll
emotional   physical   lingers   a ghost
a torturer who taunts   imagining   there is an answer
Siren's song of a cure   They still don't know what's wrong—
virus   mold   smog   chemicals—
And what if feeling better   doesn't include a cure?

Love

there will be no miracle.

Days and nights I couldn't sleep,
I walked instead,

one foot   the next,
red dust in my breath,

lungs, hair.
Pine needles. Pine scent.

Moon a gaping mouth.
Time moved slowly.

And there, sometimes,
a deer

entirely white except
a stain of pink inside each ear,

hooves dusted red.
Like fog, hovering—

To love bare limbs,
thin arms reaching.

To love new leaves in bloom.
To love their death,

layering of brown, orange,
too-late green.

To love toppling,
growth rings exposed.

To taste sweet pull of sap,
bark's thickening.

Mouth filled with golden light.
To want to call my own—

And what if I asked

for the willow's branches

again to braid its leaves?

Love

Pain changes us—

nights I couldn't sleep,
imagined blades cutting flesh

from flesh, serrated edge—

your hand on mine
and all I wanted—

      ashes to
      ash tree—

Nights I lay awake—

part crying out, part inhaled breath—

and everything we touch—

Love

We are the sum of our

biochemical wilderness
diet
exercise
DNA
subtle hormone variation
broken alarm signaling—

And what of

estrogen
radiation
abnormal response to stimuli?

What of the garden's plan?

The dove made a mistake—

Before the rain :

a hazy, deadened sky
damp with its own desire

to break. All day, building.
Wind shook the window frames.

All day, prescriptions filled
unfilled, pills swallowed,

flushed down the drain.
All day, a waiting room :

      plastic chairs
      industrial carpet
      year-old magazines.

A body in pain.

Waiting—

lattices of tissue   muscle   ligament
cacophony of blossoming   *arborescent*   nerve tree
no miracle   too late   specialists
in state after state   *Siren's song of a cure*   cysts
the size of peas   almonds   apricots
knife point   blade   time moved slowly

                              No one healthy can understand—

A body in pain—
        say it—

my body—

        breasts
        hips
        feet—

My body

        walking
        away.

In the red pine grove,
air heavy, sap-sweet, red dust

through mottled branches,
air in my lungs reddening.

All day, building.

Until
one long, loud crack :

lightning.
And the sky opened.

And there :

      a deer

entirely white except
a stain of pink inside each ear.

Like fog, hovering.

Years
I couldn't sleep—

     Pain changes us—

Years I longed
for my own release—

     Take this body, make it whole—

Time moved slowly.

And then I walked away,
stood in a grove of red pine trees.

And the sky opened,
something like relief.

And my skin began to harden
into bark, woody veins,

my arms a crown of limb and
leaves that breathe,

my heart's four chambered walls,
growth rings.

Pain washed away in sudden streams—

What is remembered in the body—

       salicin   aspirin—

       part crying out, part inhaled breath—

Crows flew to my new leaves,
nestled in my canopy.

Queen Anne's lace
gathered itself, bouquet.

Love

My body in pain.
Waiting.

And then I left it.
Turned myself to tree.

Biographical Note

Andrea Scarpino is the author of the poetry collection *Once, Then* (Red Hen Press, 2014), and the chapbook *The Grove Behind* (Finishing Line Press, 2009). She received a PhD in Creative Writing from Bath Spa University, and an MFA from The Ohio State University. She serves as Poet Laureate of Michigan's Upper Peninsula (2015–2017) and has been published in numerous journals including *The Cincinnati Review*, *Los Angeles Review*, *PANK*, and *Prairie Schooner*. She lives in Marquette, MI.